365 DAYS OF DAILY ENCOURAGEMENTS FOR MARRIED COUPLES

A. C. BOWIE

For Nathan and Gaby - may you always be motivated to keep your marriage sweet!

INTRODUCTION

When I started this project, my husband suggested I wrote a book entitled Weekly Encouragements for Married Couples so I would only have to come up with fifty two and not three hundred and sixty five top tips. My office boss also said the same thing. But I was determined and undaunted by the task until I got to Day 47... when I ran out of inspiration!

Therefore this book consists of the following encouragements and advice:

(1) those made up out of my own head
(2) quotes straight from the Bible
(3) from the leadership team and other friends from International Harvest Church
(4) from my colleagues at work
(5) from various marriages websites and Instagram pages
(6) from my husband Andrew

After a while, it became clear that the following themes came up repeatedly but were expressed in lots of different ways and I found it fun to read the different ways:

(1) Communication
(2) Household duties
(3) Spiritual lives
(4) Values
(5) Vision
(6) Interests
(7) Physical intimacy
(8) Romance
(9) Navigating conflict
(10) Navigating hard times
(11) Celebrations
(12) Navigating differences
(13) Wider family
(14) Children
(15) Finances

It became a truly collaborative effort and you will read the names of the many people who offered their tips in the Acknowledgements. I hope the book serves its purpose and is the inspiration to keep finding ways to keep your marriage sweet!

Day 1

Tell your spouse "I love you" everyday and as many times as you like...

Day 2

Serve one another. Make it the joy of your life to serve one another.

Day 3

Pray together - morning and night. Fight for it (but don't fight about it!).

Day 4

Honour your spouse with your words when you speak about them to others.

Day 5

Life is brief - quickly forgive.

Day 6

Go to bed at the same time whenever possible.

Day 7

No secrets - only birthday surprises!

Day 8

Eat meals together - at a table preferably.

Day 9

Don't expose or humiliate your spouse - they don't like it.

Day 10

Thank your spouse when they do something considerate for you.

Day 11

Be the first to say sorry. And say sorry properly along the lines of 'I'm sorry for .... Will you forgive me?'

Day 12

Do hard jobs together. But if you can't do them together YOU do the hard job anyway..

Day 13

Don't bear grudges.

Day 14

Kiss your spouse goodbye and kiss them when you see them again.

Day 15

Be accountable to one another. Practise!

Day 16

Physical intimacy is a form of spiritual warfare and brings deep connection.

Day 17

Try saying "I love you" to your spouse in another language.

Day 18

Don't nag - it doesn't work.

Day 19

Send your spouse an encouraging/romantic/flirtatious phone message.

Day 20

Make up reasons to celebrate.

Day 21

If your spouse has a brilliant (but unworkable) idea, don't be too quick to burst that idea bubble. Or at the very least, be diplomatic!

Day 22

Seeking outside help if things are hard is not weakness, it's called fighting for your marriage.

Day 23

Spend time with your favourite married couples and get *their* top tips for keeping marriage sweet.

Day 24

Have you decided a spending budget? Stick to it. And if you haven't stuck to it, 'fess up quick. The quicker the better.

Day 25

Be the one who picks the yucky stuff out of the sink today.

Day 26

Buy presents for your spouse that THEY like, not presents you like!

Day 27

Find a fun common goal, like the Great North Run or salsa dancing that you can do together.

Day 28

The BEST common goal is to serve God together.

Day 29

Be patient with your spouse because love is patient.

Day 30

Be kind to your spouse because love is kind.

Day 31

Don't be envious of your spouse because love doesn't envy.

Day 32

Don't be boastful about how awesome you are to your spouse because love isn't boastful.

Day 33

Don't be arrogant because love isn't arrogant.

Day 34

Don't be rude, crude or vulgar with your spouse because love isn't rude.

Day 35

Don't insist on getting your own way with your spouse because love doesn't insist on getting its own way.

Day 36

Don't be irritable and grumpy with your spouse because love isn't irritable.

Day 37

Don't nurse resentment toward your spouse because love isn't resentful.

Day 38

Don't triumph in doing the wrong thing to your spouse because love doesn't rejoice at wrongdoing.

Day 39

Both of you be lovers of the truth because love rejoices with the truth.

Day 40

Bear up under hard times together because love bears all things.

Day 41

Both of you believe that God is good and is working all things together for your good because love believes all things.

Day 42

Tell your spouse that God is good on the days when they need to hear you have faith in order to help them to strengthen their faith.

Day 43

Be a couple that hopes in God because love hopes in all things.

Day 44

Be the voice of hope to your spouse on the days when they need to be strengthened in their hope because love hopes in all things.

Day 45

Be prepared to endure hardship together because love endures all things.

Day 46

When your spouse is going through hard stuff, be prepared to be the strong one even if you feel weak because love endures all things. God will help you do that.

Day 47

Everything else will come to an end but love never ends. Live and work for the things that will never come to an end.

Day 48

Make a habit of meeting and getting to know new people because it brings out the best in you which acts like an upward spiral in your lives.

Day 49

Be prepared to spend money on things that don't matter to you.

Day 50

Get used to the idea in marriage that women accumulate more hair in unexpected places over the years and men lose more of it off their head over the years in order to gain it on the ears, eyebrows, nose, nostrils and eyebrows.

Day 51

If your spouse snores, one technique is to gently rub their chest or arm, another is to gently say 'ssssshhhhhh'. If that doesn't work delete the word 'gently' and try again!

Day 52

Bodily noises are natural but it doesn't excuse you from saying 'pardon me' afterwards.

Day 53

Timing is everything when raising some subjects with your spouse.

Day 54

Just clear up after your spouse and don't keep score of it.

Day 55

Accept that you are both putting in 100% into the marriage.

Day 56

Don't assume. Always ask - especially about motives.

Day 57

What seems obvious to you isn't to your spouse - so be prepared to try something a different way.

Day 58

Timing is everything when raising some subjects. Straight after work is never usually the best time.

Day 59

Your spouse may be more right than you think!

Day 60

If you have agreed a 'pocket money' limit, stick to it.

Day 61

No mobile phones at meal times.

Day 62

Always remember to laugh.

Day 63

Speaks encouraging words to your spouse.

Day 64

Think the best of your spouse.

Day 65

Think of something you love about your spouse every day.

Day 66

Thank God for your spouse.

Day 67

Take out the bins.

Day 68

Pull the accumulated hair out of the plug hole of the shower.

Day 69

Don't fixate on the little things.

Day 70

Play and have fun together!

Day 71

Make the effort for one another.

Day 72

Never go to bed angry - try and solve it before going to bed. But if it's late, resolve to solve it in the morning.

Day 73

Make time to invest in your relationship.

Day 74

Make time to invest in yourself - that will ultimately benefit your spouse.

Day 75

Revisit the places you used to go when you first started dating.

Day 76

Listen well - seek to understand.

Day 77

Try not to personalise.

Day 78

When your spouse asks you to do something, do it as quick as you can.

Day 79

Always remember to date your spouse.

Day 80

Take photos of the special occasions.

Day 81

You're most likely to be a little bit to blame.

Day 82

Try to win the person not the argument.

Day 83

If you're playing a board game, don't bring up who won last time, especially if it was you!

Day 84

The same goes for sport (see Day 83).

Day 85

Celebrate month-a-versaries.

Day 86

Celebrate the baby steps in your relationship.

Day 87

Don't shout.

Day 88

In a disagreement, focus on the issues and not on insulting your spouse.

Day 89

If you're going to eat garlic, the law of the Medes and the Persians is that both of you need to eat garlic.

Day 90

Always have a handy supply of mints to make sure your breath is always fresh - you never know when you might need to kiss your spouse!

Day 91

Bear in mind when you marry your spouse, you also 'marry' their family too (kind of).

Day 92

Children are a fulfilment of marriage, not a distraction from it.

Day 93

Handwritten notes or letters are a very romantic form of communication.

Day 94

There is some evidence that marriage reduces the risk of diabetes.

Day 95

Don't spend too much time on your smart phones.

Day 96

Try and go a walk together at least once a week.

Day 97

Don't worry if your spouse is an enigma to you - you have the rest of your life together to figure them out.

Day 98

You will bless your spouse if you fill up the car with fuel.

Day 99

Make up special occasions.

Day 100

Go for a picnic in the bandstand of the local park.

Day 101

Go for long walks together just to enjoy chatting together without the distraction of screens.

Day 102

No phones at mealtimes or bedtime.

Day 103

Work is never more important than your relationship.

Day 104

Say sorry, even when you think you're right - it will usually prompt your spouse to do so as well.

Day 105

Discuss the things that are important to you and where you don't see eye to eye, try to find compromises.

Day 106

Encourage one another to find and pursue hobbies together and independent of one another.

Day 107

Always be willing to cancel plans made elsewhere if your spouse needs emotional support.

Day 108

Talk together about to divide up the housework.

Day 109

Procrastination and impatience do not make for a happy couple, while patience and promptness are happily wed.

Day 110

Sometimes your spouse needs their own space, and that's ok. It doesn't mean they don't want to spend time with you ever again.

Day 111

Some times when your spouse is complaining, they're not looking for you to solve their problems, they just want you to listen and offer sympathy.

Day 112

If you ever feel like a problem is too big to overcome, consider that other people have come through similar problems and can't even remember them after a few years.

Day 113

Try to understand your spouse's temperament.

Day 114

Try to understand your own temperament and why you react the way you do.

Day 115

Be curious not furious eg "I'm curious to know why you reacted like that - can you help me understand?"

Day 116

Take a genuine interest in what interests your spouse.

Day 117

Identify your spouse's strengths and honour and affirm them.

Day 118

Understand your spouse's weaknesses and come to peace about them.

Day 119

Pray for your spouse every day.

Day 120

Ask your spouse how you can pray for them.

Day 121

Create a shared vision for your marriage together.

Day 122

Dream about the kind of marriage and home you want to build together and think of how you can both make it happen.

Day 123

Talk about the kind of legacy that you want to leave behind as a couple.

Day 124

Talk about the strong and weak points of your respective parents' marriage - what you would like to emulate and what you wouldn't want to repeat in your marriage.

Day 125

Learn how to resolve a conflict.

Day 126

Seek to be friends with your spouse.

Day 127

Do all you can to build trust with your spouse by being reliable, keeping your word, doing what you promised you would do and being careful around anyone who might tempt you to do the wrong thing.

Day 128

It's ok to agree to disagree.

Day 129

Your spouse is human just like you - shock!

Day 130

Your spouse can never be the Messiah for you nor Superman/Superwoman - you both need a Saviour, his name is Jesus.

Day 131

Never take one another for granted.

Day 132

Accept your spouse for who they are - they will change over time - but not in your time!

Day 133

Keep intimacy alive in your marriage.

Day 134

Don't try to control your spouse.

Day 135

Let go of the fantasy - marriage takes effort and it won't be perfect but it can still be beautiful.

Day 136

Never threaten to leave in a moment of anger or frustration - it sows seeds of insecurity.

Day 137

Respect each other in public and in private.

Day 138

Marriage is always having someone pity-laugh at your jokes!

Day 139

Marriage is not only about marrying the right person, it's BEING the right person.

Day 140

Cultivate a good sense of humour.

Day 141

Face the world and its challenges together.

Day 142

Develop a plan to build a strong foundation in your marriage.

Day 143

Make your spouse a cup of tea or coffee in the morning.

Day 144

Have reasonable and realistic marriage expectations.

Day 145

Be selective about who you share your troubles with.

Day 146

Honour your spouse when with friends.

Day 147

Learn from those married couples who practise what they teach.

Day 148

Talk about your financial goals.

Day 149

Practise hospitality.

Day 150

Having people round for a meal doesn't have to be costly - a pasta bake made with love is a princely meal!

Day 151

Set up different bank accounts for different spending purposes, for example, food, utility bills, pocket money etc.

Day 152

Set up a giving account because Jesus said "'It is more blessed to give than receive" (Acts 20:35).

Day 153

Light candles when you eat a meal and it instantly becomes romantic.

Day 154

Lie on the settee together.

Day 155

Stick a map on your dining room table and then you and your spouse can dream about the places you want to visit.

Day 156

Listen without interrupting.

Day 157

Always find a reason to hug.

Day 158

Speak without accusing.

Day 159

Answer without arguing.

Day 160

Give ungrudgingly.

Day 161

Forgive without punishing.

Day 162

Promise without forgetting.

Day 163

Comfort your spouse when they are discouraged.

Day 164

If you have to travel and be away from one another, maintain good contact with your spouse.

Day 165

Be good news for your spouse.

Day 166

Do a random act of kindness for your spouse.

Day 167

Make a couples bucket list together.

Day 168

Take a shower together.

Day 169

Don't interrupt your spouse when they are concentrating on a task.

Day 170

If your spouse is frustrated and upset, do the things that will calm them and help them.

Day 171

Comfort your spouse when they are discouraged.

Day 172

Tell your spouse what you find attractive about them.

Day 173

Let your spouse clean their way, not your way...
 ...maybe you could learn a thing or two from your spouse.

Day 174

Give your spouse a massage.

Day 175

Have an afternoon nap with your spouse ...

Day 176

Speak well of your spouse's family.

Day 177

Don't let disagreements linger.

Day 178

Flirt with your spouse.

Day 179

Your words are powerful.

Day 180

Call to mind why you fell for your spouse in the first place.

Day 181

Reminisce about the things you did when you first got together.

Day 182

Reminisce about the highlights of your honeymoon.

Day 183

Be a team.

Day 184

Be prepared to change.

Day 185

You are not the Holy Spirit - don't try to do his job - let God do what only God can do.

Day 186

Apologise quickly.

Day 187

Focus on taking the planks out of your own eye.

Day 188

Laughter can get you through the difficult days.

Day 189

Don't be over-sensitive, try not to get easily offended.

Day 190

Tell your spouse that joke you heard at work today.

Day 191

Make every event in the day seem like an exciting story to recount to your spouse at night.

Day 192

Unless requested, don't write task lists for your spouse.

Day 193

After passing wind in bed, don't stick your spouse's head under the covers - they might suffocate...

Day 194

If you bed in pray together at night, don't pray too long or your spouse may fall asleep.

Day 195

Asking clarifying questions during movies apparently is annoying.

Day 196

Become fluent about how you're *really* feeling - hunger and tiredness are not real emotions and anger is often a mask for sadness and disappointment. Why are you sad or disappointed?

Day 197

If you're tired of asking "how was your day?", ask "what good thing happened today?" or "did anything unexpected happen today?"

Day 198

Make every day count.

Day 199

Praise your spouse to your friends, colleagues and family.

Day 200

Don't be shy about initiating physical intimacy with your spouse.

Day 201

Send a real letter to your spouse - what a treat to get a real letter through the post!

Day 202

Hold hands with your spouse in bed.

Day 203

It's not your job to 'complete' your spouse.

Day 204

Share the driving.

Day 205

Love your in-laws.

Day 206

Do mundane tasks together.

Day 207

Keep one another's secrets, but don't keep secrets from one another.

Day 208

Own your own issues.

Day 209

Learn how to lose an argument with grace.

Day 210

Respect one another's privacy.

Day 211

Don't fall out in public.

Day 212

No sulking.

Day 213

Accept your differences.

Day 214

Teach and be teachable.

Day 215

Cook for one another.

Day 216

Work on making yourself an easier person to live with.

Day 217

Watch your tone of voice.

Day 218

A usual routine can be comforting and reassuring. Spontaneous injections of fun can keep life vibrant.

Day 219

Even if you know best, ask your spouse. You will probably be freshly surprised by a different perspective.

Day 220

Find a tune or food, make it your own and memories will flood back every time you hear or taste it again.

Day 221

Even when you have to deal with some of the heavy things that life throws at you, keep it light with humour that helps you both smile through it.

Day 222

Be nice to each other.

Day 223

As time goes by, love gets stronger and stronger and deeper and deeper.

Day 224

Talk about your parenting styles before you have children and continue to do so when you become parents.

Day 225

Nothing can bring a real sense of security into the home except true love.
　Billy Graham

Day 226

Above all, love each other deeply, because love covers a multitude of sins.
　1 Peter 4:8

Day 227

Great marriages don't happen by luck or by accident. They are the result of a consistent investment of time, thoughtfulness, forgiveness, affection, prayer, mutual respect, and a rock-solid commitment between a husband and a wife.
    Dave Willis[1]

Day 228

Your marriage is the gospel you are preaching to your children.
    Matthew L. Jacobson

Day 229

Every love story is beautiful, but ours is my favourite.
    Unknown

Day 230

I want my life and my marriage to look less like the world and more like Christ.
  Marquis Clarke

Day 231

It's not the love that sustains the promise, it's the promise that sustains the love.
  Darlene Schacht

Day 232

What therefore God has joined together, let no man separate.
  Mark 10:9

Day 233

What you are facing is intended to strengthen your marriage, not destroy it.
    Jackie Bledsoe

Day 234

Marriage is a mosaic you build with your spouse. Millions of tiny moments that make up your story.
    Jennifer Smith[2]

Day 235

God's Word is the perfect guidebook for marriage, and those who live by His Word will reap the blessings that obedience brings.
    Darlene Schacht[3]

Day 236

A happy marriage is the union of two good forgivers.
　Ruth Bell Graham

Day 237

Oh darling, let's be adventurers!
　Unknown

Day 238

Be completely humble and gentle; be patient, bearing with one another in love.
　Ephesians 4:2

Day 239

A marriage cannot survive when we think only of ourselves. We need to recognise that to love someone is a choice, not a feeling.
    Christin Slade[4]

Day 240

A good marriage isn't something you find: it's something you make and you have to keep on making it.
    Gary Thomas[5]

Day 241

Though one may be overpowered, two can defend themselves. A cord of three strands is not quickly broken.
    Ecclesiastes 4:12

Day 242

Marriage is sharing your life with your best friend, enjoying the journey along the way, and arriving at every destination... together.
    Fawn Weaver[6]

Day 243

Your marriage is a gift - not just to the two of you, but to this world.
    Aaron and Jennifer Smith[7]

Day 244

The happiness of married life depends upon making small sacrifices with readiness and cheerfulness.
    John Seldon

Day 245

God has set the type of marriage everywhere throughout the creation. Every creature seeks its perfection in another. The very heavens and earth picture it to us.
   Martin Luther

Day 246

There is no more lovely, friendly or charming relationship, communion or company, than a good marriage.
   Martin Luther

Day 247

As God by creation made two of one, so again by marriage He made one of two.
   Thomas Adams

Day 248

Marriage was ordained for a remedy and to increase the world and for the man to help the woman and the woman the man, with all love and kindness.
William Tyndale

Day 249

Let the wife make the husband glad to come home, and let him make her sorry to see him leave.
Martin Luther

Day 250

Let marriage be held in honour among all, and let the marriage bed be undefiled, for god will judge the immoral and adulterous.
Hebrews 13:4

Day 251

When I have learnt to love God better than my earthly dearest, I shall love my earthly dearest better than I do now.
    C.S. Lewis

Day 252

The most important thing a father can do for his children is to love their mother.
    Henry Ward Beecher

Day 253

Many marriages would be better if the husband and the wife clearly understood that they are on the same side.
    Zig Ziglar

Day 254

There's no sense in improving your marriage until you are secure with God.
Francis Chan

Day 255

A successful marriage requires falling in love many times, always with the same person.
Mignon McLaughlin

Day 256

In Christian marriage, love is not an option. It is a duty.
R.C. Sproul

Day 257

According to the Bible, the marriage act is more than a physical act. It is an act of sharing. It is an act of communion. It is an act of total self-giving wherein the husband gives himself completely to the wife, and the wife gives herself completely to the husband in such a way that the two actually become one flesh.
    Wayne Mack

Day 258

God speaks with authority on every subject including marriage and His advice trumps Oprah's every time.
    Kirk Cameron

Day 259

God created marriage. No government subcommittee envisioned it. No social organisation developed it. Marriage was conceived and born in the mind of God.
Max Lucado

Day 260

Love me when I least deserve it, because that's when I really need it.
Neil Gaiman

Day 261

I am my beloved's and my beloved is mine.
Song of Solomon 6:3

Day 262

Marriage is getting to have a sleep over with your best friend, every single night of the week.
   Christie Cook

Day 263

Ladies, a real man does more than pay for you, he prays for you.
   Jarrid Wilson

Day 264

Have a good and godly marriage that shows the world Christ's love through how you sacrificially love and serve one another.
   John Stange

Day 265

Only when marriage and family exist for God's glory and not to serve as replacement idols are we able to truly love and be loved. Remember, neither your child nor your husband (or wife) should be who you worship, but instead who you worship with.
Mark Driscoll

Day 266

Before your marriage, the enemy does everything he can to illicitly bring you together in physical intimacy and after marriage he does everything he can do to drive you apart and stop you from being physically intimate. So if you want to resist the devil in marriage, you know what you have to do!

Day 267

Not all problems need a solution but perhaps a sympathetic ear and a hug instead.

Day 268

Marriage is a bank account that is well-worth keeping topped up.

Day 269

No matter how many rules we make for ourselves, rules don't create godly relationships. Only leaning on our faithful Father and longing to please Him with everything we do will set the stage for a beautiful romance.
   Eric Ludy

Day 270

He who finds a wife finds a good thing and obtains favour from the Lord.
   Proverbs 18:22

Day 271

Therefore a man shall leave his father and his mother and hold fast to his wife, and they shall become one flesh.
   Genesis 2:24

Day 272

But now these three remain: faith, hope and love. But the greatest of these is love.
   1 Corinthians 13:13

Day 273

Satan likes to exaggerate your spouse's flaws and mistakes, to get you to focus on reasons why you should be upset.[8]

Day 274

The act of sexual union between husband and wife is like a regular renewal of your vows.

Day 275

Praying blessing for your spouse and thanking God for your spouse during physical intimacy is the best way to dispel unhelpful thoughts and/or distractions.

Day 276

Do something that your spouse likes/enjoys.

Day 277

Make time for a date night - be creative, it doesn't have to cost much.

Day 278

Share what you've read from your devotionals.

Day 279

Don't assume your spouse knows what you're thinking - they're not mind readers!

Day 280

Always assume that each other's actions (no matter how they appear) come from right motives.

Day 281

Don't be afraid to challenge and call each other to account, but do so in love and at the appropriate time (first forgive and deal with any hurt in your heart before confronting; don't use accusatory language eg "you did this…", frame things as a question or as an expression of how you feel/felt).

Day 282

Your spouse deserves a massage.

Day 283

A godly marriage doesn't happen by accident. You have to be intentional and keep God at the centre.[9]

Day 284

Marriage is better when it's built off purpose, not just passion. Lust fades. Finances or health may dwindle. Looks may even fade, but a couple that loves one another and is focused on God will overcome any season.[10]

Day 285

Your spouse is your partner, not your problem. Don't try to fix them. Don't think arguing will help them grow or feel safe. Be their prayer partner, business partner and biggest cheerleader. Take a stand together and God will keep you.[11]

Day 286

Being tired is not a competition - you are both allowed to feel tired and you both need rest even if one of you has been up all night (e.g. with a baby!).

Day 287

Apologise first even if you feel more wronged.

Day 288

Understand that either you or your spouse will be blind to different types of mess in the house and that it takes time and grace to address this.

Day 289

Be your best self at home.

Day 290

Continue to give thoughtful surprises.

Day 291

Worship together.

Day 292

Be kind to each other's families.

Day 293

Compliment each other often - be intentional about this as it's easy to let slide!

Day 294

Understand the way your parents did it may not be the way your own family should do it.

Day 295

If your spouse asks you to do something for them, even something minor, try to do it straight away and with a smile :)

Day 296

When you leave the house together, even if you're rushing or late, don't leave your spouse behind while you get in the car or go to the gate - wait for them and walk together.

Day 297

Wherever you are in the house and whatever you're doing, try to come and meet your spouse at the door when they come in from being away for a few hours e.g. shopping, work etc.

Day 298

Whenever you think "it drives me crazy when…" your spouse does something irritating, immediately follow it up in your mind with "but I love that because…".

Day 299

The depth of your closeness to each other is directly related to the depth of your relationship with God.

Day 300

Do things together - as many things as possible.

Day 301

Keep finding and developing common interests. It gives you more things to chat about.

Day 302

Touch often and always, even when you've quarrelled.

Day 303

Adopt each other's friends.

Day 304

Encourage each other to make new friends - you need those 'others'.

Day 305

Keep your vows somewhere handy and on difficult days, take them out and remind yourself of the promises you made to one another.

Day 306

Go on road trips together. Car journeys are great places to connect with one another and it creates time to have the in-depth conversations you need that build a strong marriage.

Day 307

'Don't let the sun go down on your anger' is good counsel but it isn't always feasible to sort everything out before the 'sun goes down' so call a truce and make time the next day to sort out the conflict.

Day 308

Couples who pray together stay together.

Day 309

Covenant is the safest and most beautiful thing that there is under the sun.[12]

Day 310

If you don't book in a date or time with your spouse, it will very quickly get booked out.

Day 311

Celebrate your big anniversaries in an as extravagant way as possible. These are significant milestones in your married life together and ought to be marked and remembered.

Day 312

Go whisper in your spouse's ear "I'm glad I'm married to you!".

Day 313

Remember that, under God, marriage is your first vocation.

Day 314

You have the potential to make each other very happy or very miserable. Choose happy.

Day 315

Eat together, even if one of you is late in.

Day 316

Sit down at the table to eat.

Day 317

Do the crossword together.

Day 318

Learn to play Piquet.[13]

Day 319

Pray to love your spouse more.

Day 320

You are King and Queen of a little kingdom. Feel the dignity.

Day 321

Exercise hospitality.

Day 322

Go for walks.

Day 323

If you need to talk about a big issue, go on a silent retreat together. God will sort it out.

Day 324

Choose a motto for yourselves.

Day 325

Fear the Lord above all things - it will serve as the bungee cord that will keep pulling both of you back into His ways and purposes and it will help prevent 'drift' in your marriage.

Day 326

Don't be afraid to lovingly confront when problems arise otherwise the problem may become a ticking time bomb.

Day 327

If you feel you have to confront your spouse do it humbly and gently saying things like "Can you help me understand..." or "I've been thinking a bit more about..." or "I'm worried about this..."

Day 328

Don't leave kitchen cupboards open and crumbs on the worktop!

Day 329

Kiss every morning. Men who kiss their wives every morning earn 30% more than those who don't!

Day 330

Find a way of discussing any problems or issues without criticising each other. Make it an appeal about 'us' being better rather than about 'you' ie. about your spouse needing to change. Don't get defensive.

Day 331

Always go to bed at the same time as each other. (Don't get into the habit of one of you staying up later on your own).

Day 332

Pray together daily even if it's just for a minute or two. Start with speaking a blessing over each other in the morning for the day ahead.

Day 333

Never leave wet towels on the floor... wipe round the bathroom sink after you've used it... and put the toilet seat down!

Day 334

Avoid using 'aways' or 'never' in a negative context, as in 'you always...' or 'you never...'

Day 335

Have an amount that you agree between you that it's ok to spend on something without discussion. Don't go over this without talking. (It's usually small when you're starting out!)

Day 336

Don't let your wife be in the 69% of women who do most or all of the housework! And don't let your husband be in the mistaken 97% who think they do enough!

Day 337

It's better to lose any argument but win a heart.

Day 338

Believe the best of each other, don't assign poor motives to each other, cover each other's backs and never make a joke in front of others that shows your spouse in a poor light.

Day 339

Have fun together! "Enjoy the wife (and husband) of your youth" Ecclesiastes 9:9. Keep and work at a sense of romance and adventure in your relationship. Don't wait until you think you can afford this, just get creative!

Day 340

If the grass ever looks greener on the other side of the fence, water your own backyard!

Day 341

If people tell you that must always resolve every dispute or argument before going to sleep as in "don't let the sun go down on your anger" (Ephesians 4:26) totally ignore them!

It doesn't say resolve everything, it just says don't end the day angry! So choose to stop being angry, have a cuddle and get a good night's sleep. Then you can talk about things in the daylight (they always seem better and less important then anyway). Our rule is never talk about anything significant or conflictual after 10pm.

Day 342

There is absolutely nothing wrong with a companionable silence when spending time with your spouse.

Day 343

It's better to communicate that you don't like the meal your spouse has cooked otherwise they may make it repeatedly thinking you like it. However, it's important to find a diplomatic way to say that like "it's not my favourite" or "I wasn't overly keen on that".

Day 344

Find out whether your spouse is a morning person or a night owl. Your spouse may really appreciate peace and quiet in the morning so being overly chatty in the morning may not bless them. Alternatively your spouse may want to fall asleep straight away in bed and may not appreciate when you have 10,000 more words to speak.

Day 345

Really, really, really think through getting a dog before getting one especially if it's before having children.

Day 346

Always find time and space in that secret place of intimacy to show your spouse how much you love them.

Day 347

Make sure your breath always smells sweet.

Day 348

Find and maintain your relationship with God and that will keep your relationship with your spouse right.

Day 349

Smile.

Day 350

Treat your spouse with respect. Even if you're a big shot in your workplace, don't be like that at home.

Day 351

There is always a solution for every problem and challenge you will face.

Day 352

Learn your spouse's life language/love languages.

Day 353

Don't forget to give gifts, even if they are small or simple.

Day 354

Never stop making the effort for each other.

Day 355

Buy a birthday calendar and write down all all the significant birthdays. Don't assume it's the responsibility of your spouse to remember important birthdays!

Day 356

Buy a birthday calendar and write down all all the significant birthdays. Don't assume it's the responsibility of your spouse to remember important birthdays!

Day 357

Pursue the 'God' life not the 'good' life.

Day 358

On the days when you don't 'feel' it, just do what you would normally do on the days when you do.

Day 359

It's more important to create good memories than take good pictures.

Day 360

Marriage is for richer and for poorer.

Day 361

Marriage is for in sickness and in health.

Day 362

Delight yourself in your spouse's hobbies.

Day 363

Be a good influence on your spouse. Make them want to be a better person.

Day 364

Don't lead your spouse astray by encouraging each another to be lazy or offended or bitter. Do the opposite - spur each other on!

Day 365

Together walk by faith and not by sight and then you'll be able to look back and see how far you've come as a couple.

Day 366 (For Leap Years)

Stop and remember the first time you met your spouse and share your memories of that time with each another.

---

1. See pathos.com
2. The Unveiled Wife Book
3. marriageaftergod.com
4. marriageaftergod.com
5. marriageaftergod.com
6. marriageaftergod.com
7. Marriage After God: Chasing Boldly After God's Purpose for Your Life Together
8. From liveyourbestmarriage Instagram page
9. godlydating101 Instagram page
10. godlydating101
11. godlydating101 Instagram page
12. Moral Revolution Instagram page
13. A very complicated card game.

ACKNOWLEDGMENTS

I am grateful to the following people who freely offered their top tips for keeping their marriages sweet:
John and Gillian Kamara
Andy and Antonia Charlton
Caroline Foreman
Joe and Carrie Kibbler
Emmanuel and Busola Eshiet
Paul and Fungying Koshy
Paul and Anna Carrielies
Adam and Jane Carrielies
Doug and Lily Graham
Andrew and Alison Wood
Rhys and Esther Curnow
Nathan Batten
Angus Saul
Brian Watson
Johnny Patterson
Robert Drennan
Andrew and Rosalind Starkie
Clive and Sally Harding
John and Gabby Villegas
George and Dot Rutherford

If I haven't named you and you offered free advice, please forgive my forgetfulness.

Last and definitely not least thanks to Andrew Bowie

who also offered advice and we will spend the rest of our married life together putting into practice all these excellent tips.

Printed in Great Britain
by Amazon